Wisdom from a Turtle

Wisdom from a Turtle

Thirty-Something Years
of
Seemingly Unimportant Decisions

Michael McWilliamson

iUniverse, Inc.
Bloomington

Wisdom from a Turtle
Thirty-Something Years of Seemingly Unimportant Decisions

iUniverse books may be ordered through booksellers or by contacting:

iUniverse
1663 Liberty Drive
Bloomington, IN 47403
www.iuniverse.com
1-800-Authors (1-800-288-4677)

ISBN: 978-1-4620-0257-3 (sc)
ISBN: 978-1-4620-0258-0 (ebk)

Library of Congress Control Number: 2011913964

Printed in the United States of America

iUniverse rev. date: 11/04/2011

Art by Rahul Maitra

I am "Turtle." At least that was my nickname in high school. On my first day of ninth grade in 1987, I wore a *Teenage Mutant Ninja Turtle* T-shirt, which inspired the name. So, with that said, I am presenting you here with my limited wisdom. The bulk of this book was written during a sixteen-month period in jail—a place I never thought I would ever see. Being confined to a bathroom-sized cell for months on end makes you reflect on your life in ways the average person just isn't capable of. Together with a friend I met in jail, the coauthor and artist of this book, we spent the days talking and writing about God, the universe, and the meaning of life. The goal of this book is to amuse and enlighten the casual reader as I share some stories from my life. In these pages, I talk about the lessons I've learned from the mistakes I've made as well as conclusions I've reached from observing others and society in general. Not too many of the people I know would ever read anything thicker than a comic book, so this work is illustrated to keep the not-so-highbrow reader's attention. Although many of the concepts I talk about have been written about before, I'm hoping my unique presentation will give you a new perspective for living your life.

There is a Biblical concept about spreading good news in that when you meet someone, you may very well be the only one that person will ever meet who knows the truth. It is likewise my hope that readers will consider for themselves and perhaps share the ideas found here with those who might be living in the dark. I have read most of the Bible and I will say that it changed my faulty ways of thinking and was partially the inspiration for me to write this work. I never thought of myself as being a "bad" person, but I knowingly did unsavory things without remorse. It took one big slap upside the head (imprisonment) for me to realize that my actions had very real and enduring consequences. I knew that I could no longer live however I wanted and that all the seemingly unimportant decisions I had made—and continue to make—will affect me in this life and the next.

The concepts and ideas offered here will give the reader some mental and spiritual tools for interacting with others, such as friends, family, coworkers, and even total strangers—and the ability to better cope with life's challenges. The broader viewpoints can be found in the aforementioned Bible: Love your neighbor as yourself and such. If you do not understand your higher power (God), perhaps you should consider stealing a Bible the next time you visit a hotel. So join me as I poke fun at myself and the rest of society and let's think about deep things together.

CHAPTER 1:

Do You Still Need to Be Forgiven If You Didn't Mean It?

Growing up, I don't think there was ever a time that I truly felt comfortable with my family relationships. I can't quite explain why or how, but my little world just seemed incomplete sometimes.

Being an only child from a semi-broken home accounts for some of it, but it was more than that. When I was about seven years old, my grandparents suggested to my father that he take me to the beach for a weekend bonding experience. Spending time with my dad didn't seem like too much fun, but the trip sounded like a good idea nonetheless.

My dad and I hit the boardwalk on a nice sunny day. We played pinball and video games at the arcade, we did miniature golf, and then we got to the go-cart course. I've always loved vehicles of any kind, and this was surely to be the highlight of the trip. They were not just kiddie carts, but gasoline-powered motor cars that now, incidentally, require you to show a driver's license to rent. So we got strapped in, each in our own carts, me behind my dad. My dad turned around to me and said, "Whatever you do, don't hit me."

I made a very careful mental note not to hit him. We went around the track a few times, and it was awesome! As the flag came out, I let off the gas early in an effort to coast to a stop in plenty of time to not hit my dad. As I found out, go-carts don't really coast and the car pretty much stopped when I let off the gas, which was well before the check-in area. By this time, the carny worker was hollering at me to pull the car forward. I eased the gas pedal down. I also found out that the gas pedal on a go-cart is not very sensitive and must be pushed down almost all the way before the car moves. Needless to say, when the car started moving, it was going at about full speed. Before I could stop it again, I plowed into the back of my dad's car, which totally gave him whiplash. I think this was the first time I saw fire in another person's eyes. Before I could explain what happened in my disoriented state, my dad yanked me by the arm back to the car and home we went, traveling in silence. I couldn't believe that—even as careful as I thought I was being—I still hit my dad.

THE KARDASHIAN GIRLS WERE SHOCKED INTO SILENCE AFTER MEETING THEIR LONG-LOST SISTER OLIVE...

I felt like it was destined to happen this way and I would never earn my father's trust again. As it stood, that was the last father-son activity we ever really did together. Sure, we went bowling a few times because my father was in a league. We did some stuff with my dad's girlfriends and their kids, of course. But it was never just me and my dad again. It took six months of therapy for me to realize that this was a fairly traumatic experience for me growing up. All these years, I had felt like it was my own lack of awareness that had caused the accident and I was hopelessly incapable of doing anything right. I now understand that shit just happens and how we deal with it defines us as people and not the incident itself. Thinking about my dad's perspective, it's okay to be angry about a situation, but you have to let it go eventually.

In the Bible, a guy is talking to Jesus about forgiveness. He asks Jesus how many times he should forgive someone before giving up. Jesus replies that so long as someone is trying to do right, you should forgive that person an infinite number of times. It seems that more people would have better relationships if they actually made an effort to do right and if other people forgave them more readily when they made a mistake.

CHAPTER 2:

Think of Junk Mail as Free Scrap Paper!

My grandparents mostly raised me, and all of my needs and most of my wants were met. Although no one in the family had a particularly high income, we usually had money to buy important things as we scrimped and saved on the basics.

The junk drawer in Grandma's kitchen was full of twist ties, rubber bands, scrap paper, and anything else that could be reused.

Grandma spent many hours clipping coupons and explained to me how you could save even more if an item was on sale, but that sometimes a name-brand item on sale still cost more than the generic equivalent. Of course, we didn't compromise on some things, like Coca-Cola or Jimmy Dean sausage.

When it came to clothing, I was always a good five years behind the styles. We mostly shopped at the Salvation Army secondhand store.

Grandma even knew which days they put "new" stuff on the racks so we could go and get first pick. She figured a growing boy didn't need new clothes for play, and since I went to Catholic school, I already had a uniform for that. Grandma actually made me a pair of shorts once to wear for my eighth-grade field trip to Kings Dominion. The jams were bright orange and yellow Hawaiian print and they fit perfectly—standing up, that is. At some point during our trip to the amusement park, I bent over and they split right down the butt seam. One of the teachers had to safety pin them shut to keep my butt from showing and, in a way, it sort of ruined the day.

The next year, I was thrown into the public school system like a dog to wolves. The other kids quickly pointed out to me that things like my parachute pants were years out of style. I realized that wearing a uniform to school all the years prior had not been such a bad thing after all. Despite my vocalization of the ridicule, my father and new stepmother rarely bought me new clothes, and certainly nothing fashionable.

If I wore through a knee in my jeans, they would just iron on one of those patches. What's funny is that nowadays, most "fashionable" jeans come with the holes already in them.

I didn't complain too often about my wardrobe, but when I did, I was told that when I got a job and made big bucks, I could buy whatever I wanted. Sure enough, when I started working, I did buy a few nice things for myself.

Of course, once I was on my own and had bills and rent to pay, I did save where I could and tried to make things last. I honestly did continue to shop at the secondhand stores until I was like twenty-five—and, yes, I even knew what days they put "new" stuff on the shelves. I might have bought used clothing indefinitely, but my girlfriend at the time was a bit of a snob and insisted that I start buying new stuff because old clothing was disgusting. I mean, it wasn't like I was buying used shoes or underwear, but I could see her point.

What I didn't get was that, despite the fact that my girlfriend had a fairly low income, her tastes were generally for the very expensive. She felt that a person should always buy the best, which is a standard I also adopted, with the caveat being to buy the best that *I could afford.*

Currently, I do have some nice clothing; I have actually had many items for five or ten years. As a rule, a person does want to look good and a secret to doing so is to buy clothes that actually fit.

I have noticed that girls do really notice nice clothing, especially shoes—so I make it a point not to shop at Payless.

I think we should all make it a point to look presentable. Buy decent clothing and save where you can. Buy fewer nicer things and mix and match. Remember rules like black goes with everything, no white after Labor Day, and plaid is just plain bad.

And if you can even find any, buy clothing made in America so that you're not contributing to Chinese child labor.

In the Bible, around Matthew 6 I believe, Jesus points out how beautiful the flowers look which are made by God. He goes on to say that if God can take care of the flowers and make them look so good, He will certainly take care of His human creations even more so. Thinking about this I realize that a lot of the primping we do and the trappings we surround ourselves with are mostly in vain. The real beauty of a person comes from the inside when we reflect the face of God in our lives. Obviously you want to take care of yourself, but don't get caught up in creating an illusion of who you are as opposed to working on the inner things that matter the most.

CHAPTER 3:

"Go to School or Get an F'ing Job."

These were my father's words to me about the time I became a man at the age of eighteen. This ultimatum was followed by another, which was something like: "If you don't do either, then get the f out." Well, my dad didn't really curse like that, but some quotes need a little extra color. I went to college, but after earning a mediocre GPA my first year, dear old Dad felt my efforts weren't worth paying for and cut me loose. Yes, I could have taken school more seriously, but instead, I relied on my slightly-above-average learning abilities and coasted. At this point, my dad was married to his third wife and I had a habit of being difficult with improvised family members. I left home and wound up staying with an older woman I knew who seemed to take a liking to me.

I soon found a job as a cashier at a department store and was raking in just over minimum wage. The "free" rent I was promised by the woman I moved in with actually had a price, which I wasn't too happy to pay. I thought we were just friends, but she was lonely and wanted sex, so I reluctantly engaged her sometimes. After about six months of this, I grew restless and decided I wanted to be closer to my mom. I came up with the idea that I would "transfer" my menial position from the Washington 'burbs a couple hours north to the same store chain in a small town in Pennsylvania. I made the arrangements and moved to a tiny lopsided apartment a few blocks from my mom and started working at my new location. The following experience is actually one of the main inspirations for this book project.

I was working the customer service desk one day and a little old lady stepped up boldly to the counter and pushed a shoe box toward me. She announced, "I'd like to return these . . . they didn't last as long as I thought." Upon opening the box, I raised my eyebrows and said, "Are you serious?" She said, "Oh yes, here's the receipt!" Inside the box was a pair of canvas shoes that were torn and covered with mud. The receipt showed that they were purchased over a year prior for a price of like six dollars. I said, "Ma'am, these shoes are destroyed—returned items are supposed to be in new condition! What happened to them?" Her reply was something along the lines of she had gotten them to wear for gardening and she really felt they should have lasted longer. Longer than a year, mind you.

Having experience with old people, I remained calm and said, "But ma'am, these shoes are used—very used! Do you not feel that six dollars was a fair price to pay for garden shoes that you used for like a year?" Doing her best not to pay attention to my imploring tone, she flatly replied, "No, I'd like a refund—do I need to speak to the store manager about this?" Not wanting to deal with any more hassle than my five-dollars-per-hour wage required, I decided that the store manager should be involved and called him over. I quickly explained the situation to my superior and pushed the box of barely recognizable shoes in his direction. Taking little interest in the condition of the shoes, he instructed me to give the woman a refund—in cash, no less. With a perplexed look, I said "Sir?" He said something like the customer is always right and gave me a half smile—you know the type when you squeeze up your lips but don't show any teeth. "Yes, sir" was about all I could say. I gave that old bat her lousy six dollars and thanked her sarcastically for shopping with us.

The boss later came to me to talk about small-town dynamics. He explained that if he had refused the refund, we might have very well lost that customer to the K-Mart, just a mile or so down the road. I don't remember the exact conversation, but he said something about how in the big city where I was from, people just shopped where what they needed was on sale. The retailers had less of an inclination to satisfy customers like the one just mentioned because there would always be an endless supply of new shoppers. Likewise, there were a greater number of buyers who would abuse a store's return policy. Hence, the staff had to be stricter about their enforcement of such policies.

At the time, all I could really think about was how that old lady had bamboozled us and gotten a free pair of shoes. I've had about fifteen years to think about this and, while I still feel the woman was being unreasonable, I did learn a lesson in principles. The store manager gave her that refund not because he had to, but rather because it was his greater calling to please the customer. He rose above just doing his job and acted for the implied good of the store's reputation—even though he surely saw that the lady was basically a "bad" customer. He weighed that six dollars was not worth a confrontation that would have displeased that one shopper. Incidentally, that whole chain of crap stores went out of business a few years later.

This example can be used in a Christian connotation in at least one obvious way. By serving the greater cause of God and your faith, you can make better decisions in life that will resound for longer than just a given moment. If you knew that giving someone six dollars would change his or her mind from say jumping off a bridge or something, you would do it. Right? The Bible tells us that although we are not directly "saved" by good deeds and following God's laws, we are rewarded with "treasures" in Heaven. While I don't profess to fully understand this, I do know that I would rather lose six dollars today than see someone jump off a bridge tomorrow!

CHAPTER 4:

Not All of Us Are Called to Greatness

For much of his life, my dad was a TV repairman (and, yes, he had the ultimate set of tools). He didn't go to college, but he pursued a trade, which at the time was high tech, and it looked promising. He was always humble and afforded himself few luxuries. My father's second wife was an accountant and was about as frugal as they come, which is probably most of the reason he married her—it certainly wasn't her looks, personality, or cooking. I remember Saturday nights were usually spent bargain-hunting, ending with dinner at the seafood house, where I had to lie and say I was under twelve until I was like seventeen and started growing stubble.

Anyway, it sucked because all we bought was cheap, basic stuff—nothing cool. I kid you not—we had a veritable mountain of the cheapest toilet paper ever made in the basement—the stuff that wasn't fit for even a gas-station restroom. A couple times as a teenager, I spent the night at a friend's house. The toilet paper was thicker than the towels at my house and the towels were thicker and softer than my bedspread. My friend's family was really only middle class as well, but the difference was that they actually spent their money on nice things.

Well, you get the idea, my family always rode economy style and my father never earned more than a middle-class five-digit income. When he died, however, Dad left behind over a million dollars in cash and property. Simply by being thrifty, never overindulging, working steadily, and planning, he had accumulated a small fortune by the age of fifty-eight.

Where am I taking this? A person only needs an internal drive and some self-control to work a steady job and live within—or below—his means. Just because you can afford the luxury bath tissue doesn't mean you must buy it. Doing your grocery shopping at a quick-convenience store because it's too much trouble to go to the supermart is the way of a fool. Yes, time is money, but if you are on a tight budget, you need to take the time to save the money. Likewise, if something really matters to you, don't sell your ass short and get what you want!

During my brief stay in jail, I was able to take a group talk therapy class. The stories I heard from my fellow inmates were fairly sad—and some were even tragic. Most of these men were disadvantaged in their upbringing and it was no surprise that they lacked proper social beliefs. The most common tale was how the individual was pushed into a life of crime to support their multiple children—with multiple women, no less.

They all agreed that it was better to deal drugs and hustle than to scrape by on minimum wage. Sadly, most of them had been to jail or prison more than once—each time leaving their babies' mamas to fend for themselves. Of course, they all cried about how they wanted to be in their children's lives and how important their kids were to them. I thought of the turtle and the rabbit story and guessed that working a steady, low-paying job without time off for jail sentences would yield a better income in the long run—as well as allowing for family time that wasn't divided by bars. Not even considering issues of right and wrong, it just seemed to make more sense.

A number of these men had been shot or stabbed and had done the same to others. Some of these men seemed sincere about changing their lifestyle choices, but they all seemed to think it was society's obligation to help them change. They essentially said that without free job training and placement, they would have no choice but to go back to a life of crime. After observing these guys for several months, I realized that many of them enjoyed their "thug lives" and would only change if a better life was handed to them free of effort.

Bear in mind that I was in jail right beside these men. After a brief period of denial, I came to realize that I was no better a person than they were—God made us all equal. There really wasn't much difference other than the nature of our respective lifelong string of mistakes. I learned to better myself from the experience and was truly humbled by my circumstances. Despite all the consequences of our wrongdoings, some people continue to knowingly do wicked things till the day they die.

When Jesus was hanging on the cross, there were two other men strung up next to him. They were all dying together, but the first man chose to mock Jesus and suggested that he simply free himself if he were the true Son of God. The second man realized he was dying and resigned himself to this fate which was beyond hope. The second man asked Jesus to remember him when He came into his Kingdom and Jesus told him He would. If we could all just realize that we are in fact slowly dying in this world, perhaps we could more easily put our hope in the eternal future that Jesus promises.

CHAPTER 5:

Who's Your Daddy?

When I was very little, my parents got divorced. My mom was hooked on depressants due to a doctor's poor diagnosis and was physically unable to take care of me reliably. All my dad knew was how to work. When we went to court over custody, I was actually placed in the care of my grandparents. My dad actually lived in the house right next door to his folks, so it was still as if my father had custody since I continued to sleep there. My mom actually remarried a couple years later, which automatically extended my small family. As an only child (for seven years anyway), I had more attention than I knew what to do with—and still couldn't get enough. One thing I'll say is that, with so many good influences around me, I was never left to my own devices and managed to avoid the whole drug and alcohol experimentation phase. I'm thinking about a time when I was like ten years old and was hanging out with the son of one of my mom's friends. Within minutes of entering his house, he showed me his mom's boyfriend's gun, porn collection, and vial of heroin in rapid succession. All these things were fascinating to him as they were for adults and supposedly kept hidden from him. We went to the mall later that day and stole a bunch of toys at his suggestion. Needless to say, this kid turned out to be a real piece of work and I think he's dead now.

So many children are born into homes where they are considered a burden or maybe a welfare check at best. In the past few decades, the tendency for men to father multiple children with more than one woman with no planning at all has increased exponentially. These men sow their seeds with no intention of being a parent past the biological definition. I know a woman with two daughters who has mentioned several times that the second child was an "accident" and her life would be so much easier if she had aborted the baby. Even unspoken, feelings like this come through to offspring and affect their development. I have never met the girl, but I hear she is very overweight, and has low self-worth and as other emotional issues. If you said that a lot of girls are like that, I'd respond that there is your proof of how many parents really didn't want to be parents. So what's my point, as most of this has already been said other places in other ways? My point is that something is fucked up! Don't just accept it as "times are changing" and that's just how it is. Recognize it and look at people you know who fit this pattern and call them out!

At one point, I managed a call center. I was always hiring new workers because it was a high-turnover job. On several occasions, child-support wage garnishment letters would come my way. I was amazed at how these seemingly decent, well-spoken, well-groomed men were dodging their parental obligations. In addition, after sharing the letter with the person in question, he would feign surprise and quit the job a few days later! As a man and a Christian, I can understand many of the wicked things men do, but what piece of shit won't take care of his own? Even in the animal kingdom, a good number of species parent their young through adulthood. In fact, there are even stories of wolves or dogs raising a human baby. That would make some men worse than dogs!

I imagine few of those negligent fathers are reading this book, (unless they are in jail and have some free time), but if you know one of these types—call him out! Don't be embarrassed to say something since he's the one doing wrong. For those of you who feel like you may have been an accident, remember that, even if your parents did not plan for you, your true Father God did and he does have a plan for you.

Parents, if you put your kid in front of a TV instead of reading a book with him or her, you're missing out on having the kind of wonderful relationship that I was not blessed to have. If you turn on the television for your child and then go into the other room to get high on drugs, you're throwing two lives away. Lead by example. Don't think a baby is unaware of what you are doing. Children are like sponges and absorb what they see. Every bad habit—from cursing to nose-picking—starts at home. Try living for more than just yourself.

Hopefully, you actually got married to your partner—or at least plan to. Even if it didn't work out and you're alone, the number-one priority you should set is having God in your family—single parent or not. Just as a child recognizes its mother, a human heart will recognize its Maker and will have a much more rewarding life when we ask our Creator to guide and provide for us.

CHAPTER 6:

On Hygiene—"If Ya Stank, Wash Yo Ass!"

This is about much more than personal hygiene, but while on the subject, did you know that the olfactory nerve (sense of smell) is transmitted directly into the brain as opposed to the other senses which all have to be relayed? What you smell registers instantly in the mind and can affect your mood, for better or worse. Most people are fairly regular with their bathing habits; however, some people go out of their way to smell good. You know what I'm talking about—the heavyset woman who sits down next to you on the train who must certainly buy perfume by the gallon at Costco. Seriously, you don't smell good and it actually burns my nose and gives me a headache.

Most things are only good in small doses. It says in the Bible (Romans, I think) that if something you do annoys someone else—don't do it. Although something you do may not be evil in itself, it can be offensive. If you fart in the car and roll up the windows, you might as well have just murdered your fellow travelers. Does that sound like too harsh a comparison? Perhaps thinking in extreme Biblical standards would make us all better people.

Let's expand this concept to sight and sound. Free country or not, it's just wrong to paint your house fuchsia. Although I know several people who will argue this till they are blue in the face, making your house into an eyesore is offensive and ruins the neighborhood. Likewise, no one wants to hear your favorite song on max volume at two in the morning. This is offensive and inappropriate—unless you're picking up your crack whore from the trailer park—in which case, no one probably cares and you don't want to hear what she has to say anyway.

Being considerate of others and how your actions affect them is paramount. Simple stuff like making sure your used tissue actually lands in the trashcan and not the floor—or washing the hands you just blew your nose with before offering to shake with someone.

I briefly worked with a guy who didn't flush or wash his hands after urinating. When I confronted him, he said something about saving water and then said, "My dingaling is just as clean as anyone else's." He was actually a very smart dude, but as you see, smarts have nothing to do with courtesy. Yes, this stuff sounds funny, but many people are guilty of similar transgressions and don't realize it.

In Deuteronomy it says to dig a hole and bury your crap. Not only does the Bible benefit your soul, but it has good advice for cleanliness too!

CHAPTER 7:

You're Fired!

I've confirmed the theory that people sometimes judge another person's stability and social standing by what that person does for a living. Whenever you meet new people, one of the first questions asked of you is "Where do you work?" or "What do you do?" After having close to thirty different full-time jobs in the past twenty years—and having been fired from most of them—I've realized that what I do to earn money is fairly irrelevant to who I am. As of late, I try to think more about what a person does as a human being on a daily basis. Ask yourself what your real job is. Are you a parent, role model, customer, friend, husband, or wife? These are the jobs we should really be most concerned with, but let's take a moment to talk about your job. Maybe if you improve your work habits, other areas of your life will follow. When asked where you work or what you do, the answer should come quickly. "I work at ABC Company selling urinal cakes."

Sadly, many people become so engrossed in what they do for a living that they often identify their lives only based on their employment. "Hey, there's Neil the doctor!" "There goes Bob the lawyer!" "There's Dick, the urinal cake guy!" Okay, so you're the go-to guy for fresh men's restrooms all over town. You spend your days visiting public restrooms—leaving samples and cards. You are at the top of your game! But it's not all roses and cakes. Neil and Bob own a local watering hole called the N&B Lounge. N&B is your oldest, but also your smallest, customer. In fact, they do so little business with you that it actually costs ABC Company money to continue to service the account. You tell your friends and coworkers what a shithole N&B is. You find them an annoyance and are often rude when they call. You have even hoped that N&B would just stop calling you altogether. Even though they were your first customer when you were a junior sales rep so many years ago, you now regret ever dealing with them.

Do you see where this is going? Let's jump to the moral of this story. Years ago, you were praised for bringing back this contract with N&B your very first week on the job. You used to hang out at N&B every Friday after work. Now, you have so many contracts that you disdain the meager check you collect from N&B each month. The customer you were once proud to have won is now nothing but a nuisance. Well, shame on you for thinking that way! N&B has been loyal to you all this time, but now that you're a big shot, you couldn't care less about old Neil and Bob. This is the kind of faulty thinking I would like to help readers identify and correct. Yes, I understand you *lose* money dealing with N&B. But you were the one who gave them a discount on a long-term contract way back when in exchange for signing. Heck, you haven't set foot in the door for years, but if you think back, you'll remember the free cold beer you got every time you did. In summary, you should still be thankful for their business and your job is still to treat them as any well-paying customer. Perhaps you might even visit them in person and explain how the old contract doesn't work for ABC anymore. You just might find that they understand crazy concepts such as inflation and are willing to work with you! Just do your job to the best of your ability and, if you get fired, remember that it doesn't change who you are.

A popular Christian concept is to do everything as if you were doing it for God. Since most people are at their jobs like thirty percent of their lives, this concept should naturally include your work habits. It doesn't make sense to think that you can be a ruthless asshole all day at work and then suddenly transform into a kind and loving husband or father when you get home.

CHAPTER 8:

Best Friends Forever

Many people will refer to someone they've had only a few conversations with as a "friend." For that matter, having casual sex with someone also puts them in friend status when there are no plans to have a real relationship. "She's just a friend, you say, so what's her last name?" Of course knowing someone's last name is not required for friendship, and the meaning of the word "acquaintance" has all but been forgotten. I've come to the conclusion that agreeing to be someone's friend is on part with accepting a job. As long as you work well together, you can remain employed as a friend but after three strikes (or less), you're out. I have only a few friends, and, after years of selfishness, I finally understand that my duty to a friend is to serve his or her best interest.

In the Gospel of John, we hear Jesus speak on loving his disciples. He demonstrates his friendship by serving them and, in this case, washing their feet. Out of love and friendship, the master became the servant. In your life, think about all the people you consider to be friends. Is there anything you would deny them if they asked?

I once was reading a girl's profile on a dating website and she was babbling about how she was the type of person who would do anything for her friends—unless it was illegal. Well, okay, if a friend wants you to do something that is bad either for one or both of you, you usually need to draw the line. But what about decisions that require the lesser of two evils? I'm thinking of a Bible story where a prostitute, Rahab, helps hide some of Jesus's crew from the Roman guards. They weren't even really her friends, but she stuck her neck out for them and lied to the authorities because the guards would have imprisoned or killed these disciples had they found them. What grounds does one base friendship on? Can I say that I love all the people I call friends? Would I die for them? Or even more difficult—would I live for them?

One of the many reasons marriages fail is that we lack a core friendship with our partners. Going back to the dating website babble, many girls say "friends first." Of course, they're not actually looking for the same qualities they would in a typical friend—otherwise they'd turn up nothing but gay guys. Being a good friend should go deeper than a few commonalities, a simple attraction, or a convenient arrangement.

We've all heard the term fair-weather friend. It's easy to enjoy someone's company while having fun under no pressure. The true test is—when the chips are down—can you put someone else's needs above your own? There is no need to go into great detail here regarding one's exact obligations to a friend. Just consider everything—from telling your pal about the booger dangling from his nostril to telling him when he's had too much to drink. I can honestly say that I have very few friends and would do better spending more time focusing on the ones I have rather than making new ones.

A few years prior to my brief stint in retail, my first job was working at a hotel. At sixteen, my aptly fitting title was houseboy, and my job included everything from changing light bulbs to plunging stopped toilets. My work ethic was somewhat lacking from day one and I felt entitled to help myself to any available "fringe benefits."

On several occasions, I hosted small parties in one of the vacant rooms. During one such event, my best friend fell and busted his head on the coffee table after having too much to drink. The wound itself wasn't so bad, but there was blood all over, which scared the rest of us a good bit. One or two of us wanted to call an ambulance, but we were all afraid of getting caught with hard liquor in a place we technically shouldn't have been. I, of course, would have lost my job—if not worse—and we all would have been seriously grounded. We wound up bandaging my friend's head in a veritable turban of toilet paper and drew the festivities to a close.

Days later, we actually did wind up getting found out somehow.

In any case, the situation could have been better managed. I should have valued my friend's well-being more than a minimum wage job and sought help—regardless of the consequences to me and those who were not bleeding at the time. I seem to remember that I was holding the phone ready to call 911, but my injured friend was against it and convinced us the injury wasn't so bad.

Regardless of my actions that night, I actually got fired from the job a few months later for a totally unrelated reason.

Another time, I was talking to the maintenance man at the hotel about how great it would be if I were more popular at my high school. He suggested that I should throw a party and that he would help me. In addition to working at the hotel, my pal Pernell also worked at an apartment complex a few miles away. He said he would loan me the community clubhouse for a night and he would even buy the booze.

Since the offer was too good to pass up, I gladly accepted. We picked a day and I copied up some flyers and posted them around the school. I got my beer money together and we even found an aspiring DJ to set up the music for free. Some of my fellow classmates—people I barely even talked to—came early to help set up. To my surprise, people started showing up by the dozens at the given time and I had to get a couple guys to work the door. Miraculously, the party went off without a hitch and everyone had a good time. A bunch of people even stayed to help us clean till the early hours of the morning. I don't know exactly how many people came, but at the end of the night, I had over a thousand dollars from the five-dollar cover charge. What did I gain from this? Even though only a few dozen people actually knew it was my party—my popularity did go up some—I never became part of the in crowd.

I learned that if you do something big, make sure people know who's behind it. Life is full of successes and failures and you shouldn't be shy about partaking in either. The next lesson was learning that being a friend means sometimes sticking your neck out for someone. Pernell not only risked his job to help me, but he could have been criminally charged with providing alcohol to minors. He did all this just to help improve my life based on what I thought I wanted.

Most people would have just given me some cliché advice and told me to cheer up. I don't even think I gave him any of the profit. In fact, my stingy ass only gave the two guys working the door all night like ten dollars, partially because I thought they had already kept some of the money—that's what I probably would have done. I regret letting Pernell go to such a great risk on my account—yes, he was an adult and I was technically still a boy—but still. I know in the big picture that people buy booze for kids all the time and don't go to jail or anything, but still. I also regret that, once I left that job, I made no effort to stay in touch with Pernell.

Despite the fact that he first reached out to me, I did not value him past what he could do for me in this one instance. Being a friend in return was never of concern to me and it has taken me twenty years to acknowledge my poor character.

In John 11 of the Bible, we hear about Jesus and his friend named Lazarus. One day Jesus heard that Lazarus was sick and was asking for Him to come heal him. Jesus took his sweet time and Lazarus up and died before Jesus got there. When Jesus did finally get there, he brought Lazarus back to life from death! This miracle demonstrated to the people of that day the power of God and the value of having Jesus as a friend beyond what we think he can do for us. While we don't typically see our loved ones come back to life after dying, we can still know that Jesus is the ultimate friend. He gives us even more than we ask for and in that regard, we should strive to give our friends our best.

CHAPTER 9:

Take One for the Team

As a boy, anytime we were picking teams to play a sport, I was usually picked just about last—unless there was a fat kid with glasses around. I remember how good it felt the few times I actually caught the ball or managed to score a point. I also remember feeling bad when I fumbled the ball or failed to do my part in some way, which was usually the very next play after my accomplishment. Of course, it didn't take an afterschool TV special for me to realize that just doing the best I could was all I should worry about.

While few of us have what it takes to be a professional athlete, we will all inevitably be part of a team. Be it work or family life, we should learn our specific role and do the best that we can. We should never lower our goals because someone else on the team falls short. Often you hear how one partner cheats on the other, which therefore gives the offended party license to do the same. I used to think the same way, but now I realize that it's the team that wins or loses and that points are not gained or lost individually. We should always fulfill our duties in good faith and hope others rise to the occasion after they fall short of the goal. Instead of comparing yourself to the lowest performer, stay fast to your own standards. In addition, carefully consider your chase of glory. The higher you fall from, the more you will get hurt.

One day, I was watching some guys play basketball. One particularly aggressive player made a few shots in a row and proceeded to boast, "I'll do this all myself." He was certainly a good player, but after several more minutes of hogging the spotlight, I noticed two things. First, the opposing players left their designated counterparts to guard Mr. Superstar. Second, Mr. Superstar's teammates soon lost interest and stood by almost idle. You see, the team and the game were taken out of focus for this one man's bravado. Self-recognition is not bad in itself, but praise is best when it comes from others. Consider the good of your team. Could the team do better if you let someone else take the center? Try asking your team for feedback. Are you all in agreement as to what your role should be? Are you giving and receiving proper credit? Is someone sitting on the bench too often? Find out why and let that person in the game. Don't be afraid to humble yourself and stand in the shadows for a minute to let another shine.

In the Bible, John the Baptist had the task of paving the way for Jesus. Although John could have had earthly glory and recognition, he did what he had to do for the greater good of humanity. In fact, John was even imprisoned and beheaded for doing his job correctly. Despite those consequences, he died knowing that his team would win in the end. That is conviction!

CHAPTER 10:

The World at Your Fingertips

In theory, improvements in technology improve our lives. Such improvements are regarded by many as just another change in their lives—and we all know most people hate change.

One drawback new technology poses is that one must first learn to use it in order to benefit from it. Recall the fairly accurate comment made about the videocassette recorder, how the thing required a degree in order to program it. Everyone rushed out to buy a VCR, but many never learned how to use its main feature of convenience.

I got a little upset when so many stores implemented "self-checkout" systems. Now, instead of paying people, I was paying for a machine and had to scan and bag my items on top of it all. I saw old people struggling to figure the things out and wondered if this trend would even last. Years later, I still see frustrated old people fooling with these things—and they still haven't figured them out.

In discussing my displeasure with this change, a good friend stated that, even though these machines take away low-end cashier jobs, they create better jobs in the design, assembly, software, sales, and support of these robot cashiers. All of these new jobs pay much more than the function they replace—and there will never be a robo-cashiers union.

The message to all the displaced cashiers is simple—get some training and get a better job! For a while, I was convinced that this was the correct viewpoint, and I certainly don't have a whole lot of sympathy for people who lack the desire to better themselves. Now, however, I realize that people gotta work, regardless of their skill level.

In the national and global economies, the job exchange rate between these machines and the people they replace is not even. In fact, the machines actually require a good bit of human supervision since they jam up frequently for no apparent reason. "Remove the item from the conveyor belt." Even if the line is long, I wait in the one remaining line with a person to wait on me. Fuck the machines. Maybe we can start a national movement to randomly unplug these things to send a message.

I remember when computer games were all text and no graphics. Would today's kids even bother? A couple years later—giant square pixels came in sixteen colors. Remember the game "Combat" that came with the Atari 2600? The cover art had a cool-looking tank blowing stuff up, but when you actually played the game, your tank was like a big square with a smaller square on top. But it was new and fun, and little kids figured it out because they were motivated to do so.

Where did our child-like drive go? As an adult, I find myself standing around and getting frustrated when someone "moves my cheese" just like the old people with the robo-cashiers. We learned cell phones quickly enough because talking to people is "important" and sometimes fun. However, millions of adults have no idea how to double-click the computer mouse thingy—let alone use basic time-saving software that's been around for going on like twenty years now. Despite the intense marketing campaigns in our faces, many people put off the obvious benefits of learning something new, thinking it will not last, as I mistakenly thought about the robo-cashiers. Even if it isn't good for society as a whole, take the time to figure it out and at least decide if it's good for you as an individual.

After more than fifteen years, many people still struggle with man's latest frontier, the Internet. You'll notice that Satan, (yes, I mean the Prince of Darkness), wasted no time learning the World Wide Web and it is now full of pornography and deviance.

I sometimes think the web is another advance in technology that we could have done without. From eBay to YouTube, and all the assorted nuts and sluts, we now have twenty-four-hour access to brain-rotting material.

Children are forced to grow up faster because no amount of software can protect them from the steady stream of trash available. Porn sites compete with each other based on how lewd and vile their not-so-respective material is. I shamefully admit to once having owned and operated such a site. Despite the temporary perks of being seemingly fun—and even lucrative—I can say now that it truly stained my soul and is one of my bigger regrets in life.

The devil (who is quite real, by the way) hides behind freedom of speech, and the demons of the ACLU are on his payroll. Despite vain popular beliefs, no good comes naturally from the human heart. No matter how many laws men make, lawyers will constantly find ways to bend them. The only real law was written thousands of years ago by our Higher Power—God. Unless we acknowledge that we are flawed and try to live by His standards, we will constantly fall short and do evil. Porn on the web is a destructive force for many men and I can honestly say its powers of addiction rival any drug. In my current state of awareness, I'm amazed that there are so few advocacy groups against porn. With all the public service commercials on TV, you'd think smoking a cigarette was comparable to murder!

In regard to personal computers, did you ever read the real story about the person who calls the technical support line and they discover that the computer is not plugged in? I won't tell it—just look it up yourself unless you're too dumb to use the Internet.

I was surprised that the "Internet Appliance" wasn't more popular. People still want the hulking tower that comes with all the software they will never learn to use. I wonder if anyone has ever asked, "What kind of porn does this computer come with?"

I was thinking that the cars that stay on the road the longest are the ones with the fewest features. Many noteworthy options have became popular in my lifetime: cruise control, intermittent wipers, power seats, anti-lock brakes, traction control, keyless entry, heated seats, air suspension, and airbags. Many of these options will break in less than ten years, which (trust me) is always after the extended warranty that you paid extra for has expired. At a certain point, the cost to fix broken features might even rival the value of the car itself. Before long, many fancy cars become nothing more than a big, rolling heap of broken accessories.

Even if a car still starts and stops, most people will become discouraged with a vehicle over something seemingly insignificant, such as a broken cup holder. On a side note, it took car companies like seventy-five years to figure out people even wanted cup holders. As a result of these mostly prideful feelings, people continue to trade in five-year-old cars with a few broken options minutes after the loan is paid off.

When buying a new or used car, a person should compare his or her needs to financial restrictions. If you're financing the loan, don't buy a Cadillac when a Cavalier will meet your needs—unless you can pay it off before all the fancy features break. Don't buy a $500 car and put $2,000 worth of rims on it.

Lastly, if you are an American, consider buying an American car. Buying a foreign car does little good for our country—regardless of how many factories a company may have here. If you kept the car for ten years—like you should—what does the resale value even matter? You shouldn't need a statistical study to know in your heart that imported cars are partially behind our country's current economic condition. For that matter, there are people still living who fought for freedom against the German and Japanese. Be it five years ago or fifty, what kind of jerk-off would now let these countries profit from our nation?

In the past fifty years since we began reverse-engineering that crashed alien spaceship, (which had a cup holder by the way), electronics have been getting smaller, faster, and cheaper. Most people will remember that many televisions used to come set in a finished wood cabinet and were essentially pieces of furniture. Up until the early 1990s, a TV was a fairly big-ticket purchase and was worth fixing when it broke. Until digital picture quality was conceived, there were few improvements made over the years and people bought televisions with the intent to make them last.

For a number of years, my father was the sole proprietor of a television and electronics repair shop. He liked his job for the most part and enjoyed telling stories about the occasional TV brought in by some amigo that was packed full of roaches (bugs like the heat from the tube).

As we know, the birth of Wal-Mart and other mega-importers drove the prices of electronics down—and ultimately the quality as well. I'll spare you the economics lesson, but suffice it to say that the cost to repair a broken television soon became too close to the cost of a brand new one. My father's shop soon became a graveyard of tubes and wires because no one wanted to pay to fix something old anymore. You can see where this is going so I'll just say that, after five years or so of being in business, my dad was forced to close his operation. The old bastard that sold my dad the shop saw what was coming and bailed out just in time. In fact, I don't even think Dad broke even when it was all over. When I finally sold his test equipment on eBay, machines that once cost $3,000 would sell for $30. Since there are so few American electronics companies, I'll spare you the whole domestic argument. It pays to buy the best product you can afford and to be gentle with things. Play your part, however small, and reward manufacturers who make quality items—even if the price is high. Oh, and skip the extended warranty, as it is nothing more than a retail sales perk. It's like insuring something because you know it is cheap crap and you shouldn't have to insure everything you own. Yes, your fifty-inch LG LCD that you got for $400 will most certainly break, so just don't buy it to begin with!

Free printer with purchase! In our supposed digital age, most all people still insist on printing stuff out. Okay, I get it, so let's talk about the ink. I bought an Epson multi-thingy to scan the pictures for this book. It was fifty dollars and did everything I needed.

I also used it to print maybe a dozen color photos and the blue ink ran out. Well, even though the black ink is full, it won't let me print until I replace the blue ink cartridge. I can't even use the scanner either. WTF? So now I have to spend thirty dollars on ink so I can continue to use my fifty dollar printer. For that matter, this will happen three more times as the other cartridges run out. Good thing I have this handy pop-up window on my computer here telling me where to buy the ink online. I get it—give the razor away for free and sell razor blades.

My thoughts on this? Buy the damn extended warranty and take it back when the first ink runs out. Okay, that's not very honest, but neither is selling a printer that needs ink after a dozen pictures are printed. Option B is to take out any good ink that's left, donate the thing, and buy a new one for fifty dollars. I'm sure with all our technological advancements we'll be using the moon as a dumpsite for our trash soon—so who cares!

CHAPTER 11:

Love Your Neighbor, Not His Wife

I once talked with a gentleman who recently came to America from Ghana and the conversation turned to Western culture. I asked him how he liked his neighborhood and he said it was nice with the exception of the fact that he hardly ever talked to his neighbors and would like to get to know them better. He went on to tell me that, in Ghana, simply living next to someone was almost akin to being family. He said that if he didn't see one of his African neighbors for a day or two, he would knock on their door and check on them. He also told me that if an adult in the community got sick, a neighbor would temporarily take in any children to keep them from getting sick.

He spoke of his current neighbors as being distant and aloof. He followed this up with a few examples of how they would all actually try to avoid each other; one man took a break from mowing the lawn when he saw someone coming or going next door.

I explained that much of this could be credited to living in the Washington suburbs and that people mostly kept to themselves so as not to appear nosy. Some people even avoided neighborly friendships out of fear that a given neighbor might be too friendly and might just knock on their door all the time. We've basically been conditioned to think that a knock at the door is never a good thing.

As soon as I said this, I realized that these were my very own reasons for not knowing my neighbors. For ten years, I have lived in the same place, but never talked with anyone in the community about anything much deeper than a molehill.

I was even on the HOA for five years, but I still avoided people when I could for no apparent reason. After talking with this man, I started a friendship with a guy a few doors down (also on the HOA) and found we had a lot in common. I try to say hello at least to those I see coming and going. Of course, a major Biblical teaching is to love your neighbor as yourself. If only everyone could understand such wisdom and put it into practice, imagine what great communities we'd have!

While talking about commandments and neighbors, let's talk about the guy next door. While it is okay to appreciate his sweet sports car and smoking hot wife, consider them for what they are—blessings from God. It is wrong to covet your neighbor's blessings. Don't succumb to envy and don't praise him for his life based on status or possessions. Too often, we worship money and the things it buys. I can testify that when you put God first in your life, your needs and many of your wants will be met, so seek the Lord and not a bigger paycheck.

If you say that's easier said than done, remember that you entered this world with nothing and will leave the same way. So focus more on acquiring friends rather than possessions.

Another Biblical teaching is that no act in and of itself is a sin. In times of war, even killing is allowable. However, any act that intentionally or even indirectly offends someone is considered to be wrong. So basically, if your floodlight shines in your neighbor's bedroom window at night, if your guests park in front of his driveway, or if your dog craps on his lawn—these things need to be addressed.

Of course in some cases, despite being conscious of things and courteous to others, your efforts will not be reciprocated.

Don't get discouraged and let go of your kindness. Double your efforts toward those who fail to appreciate your decency. Decent people will be remembered when they leave this world far more than any junk they leave behind.

CHAPTER 12:

Manage This

Take a quick look in any bookstore and you will find more books on management than you could read in a decade. Since most of those books are written by persons smarter than myself, let me just share some personal experience.

After an assortment of minimum-wage jobs, I discovered that I could get paid to harass people for money in the form of a sales position. Wow! No experience needed and I could earn "top dollar." Sign me up, I said.

My first sales job was peddling encyclopedias door to door. This was a couple years before the Internet became mainstream—when people still owned and read books.

The way the job offer was presented to me was like this: I could get paid ten dollars per hour or I could earn 20 percent of each sale I made. The book set cost $2,000, (I have no idea how they convinced me people would actually pay that much), so just selling one set a week would earn me the same $400 as forty hours times ten dollars per hour. But wait, if I sold two sets, it would be $800. Whoa! The earning potential was unlimited. It all looked so simple on the dry-erase board!

Here's a tip. If you interview for a job and instead of asking you about your qualifications, they start explaining how you're going to get paid, just leave. Don't walk—run. Oh, and if it's a group interview, make sure to first shout, "This is bullshit!" and then run. That way, at least others will have had a fair warning.

Anyway, I believed the hustle and, for two weeks, the manager drove us all over the place to sell these books. During this time, I was nearly eaten by a big dog, I had a gun pointed at me, and some older lady in a trailer park solicited me for sex, which I declined as my standards used to be much higher. In these two weeks, I wound up mucking my way through two presentations and made one sale.

When payday arrived, I was told that my order had cancelled, so I had not a dime to show for my efforts. It was shocking that I could have put in so much work for nothing. What a racket. The manager sold me on the idea of getting paid for my production, leading me to believe that I would be better off. Although upset by this experience, I was now interested in sales and management.

In my early twenties, I got into telemarketing. It was appealing to me as the pay was above average, (because it's a crappy job of course), and I got to sit on my butt. Having a clear voice and being fairly well spoken, I actually did okay. In addition, I showed up to work on time and took the job seriously, which is all any manager can really hope for.

After sticking with this for close to a year, I was offered a middle-management position to run canvassers door to door soliciting home-improvement services. This new job actually paid a salary and included health benefits, so I took it pretty seriously. I read a number of books on how to be a "good manager" and motivate my team. For the most part, I kept the people above me as well as the people below me content.

Managing is always being between a rock and a hard place and the cliché I found to be true was to underpromise and overdeliver. After about a year of this, I grew restless and started looking around for a better job. I wanted more responsibility, more pay, and less actual work. I found what I was looking for in little time since it's always easy to get a new job when you already have one. I joined a smaller company with similar needs who would recognize me as a dedicated manager as opposed to a glorified worker. In my zeal to get the job, however, I had promised to "steal" my existing staff from my current job.

Both my new and old employers saw that I was just another schmuck whose ethics could be bought. For a couple thousand dollars more per year, I left and essentially betrayed those who had first introduced me to management. Perhaps if had I not been born and raised in this major metropolitan area, I might have felt more loyalty to those who first trusted me. If there were fewer jobs and fewer customers, I might not have been in such a hurry to cross to the seemingly greener grass. In conclusion, this new job lasted less than two years before the owners closed shop to try something different.

During my early working years, I was constantly jumping jobs, usually on short or forced notice. I was always one paycheck away from destitution and fearful for my survival. I was reading in the Bible how the birds don't plan and store away food, yet God still feeds them. If only I had trusted God with my career, I might not have struggled so much and could have made fewer compromises of my integrity.

CHAPTER 13:

Dirty Laundry

Some say that society is getting better, but looking at the past half century since the invention of electronic media, it looks to me as if it's getting worse. In order to keep the public's interest, the media and entertainment communities have increasingly sought decadence and the musicians, actors, writers, and journalists have delivered.

Through programming and advertising, the media has conditioned us to want instant gratification. We are taken around the world in just eighty seconds, we can satisfy our hunger past midnight, and we can save 40 percent if we make our purchase right now. We are told we need things that we previously did not know existed.

Your floors will be cleaner, your food will stay fresher, and your shirts will be whiter. It's no wonder people have attention deficit and anxiety disorders, or self-esteem and depression issues. How can we be content when our brains are constantly bombarded with the need to upgrade? The FCC is overwhelmed with content to screen and can only censor the most profane and obscene material.

Lobbyists for tobacco and firearms pale in comparison to those of the free media groups. These Whores of Babylon are constantly pushing for more sex, more profanity, and more violence—to the point that some cable programming is basically a showcase of the worst humanity has to offer.

In contrast, there are no standards at all on how "smart" our viewing experience should be. Reality TV employs personalities that appeal to the least common denominator of society.

Most of these real-life shows should offend anyone with a high school diploma. Romantic relationships are debased to sexual encounters. Friendships are reduced to misery loving company. Success is shown as money, power, and possessions. All in all, there is a total lack of Godliness on our airwaves and a total emphasis on self-reliance and material dependence. Are you thinking this is a prudish view of things? Would you believe this is all just how the times have changed? How about the truth that Satan has beguiled us into thinking all this is okay! So you're thinking that blaming the devil is the best I can do? No, I blame myself, as should you. In years gone by, the public would cry out against obscenities!

People would write letters, make phone calls, stage public protests, or even boycott companies and organizations that supported wrongdoing. When I was young, I remember more than one instance of a commercial being pulled from the air or a product removed from the shelf.

Many news programs used to start and end with a happy story—a dog saving someone's life or something about a panda bear at the zoo. These feel-good stories were a response to the public outcry that news was nothing but crime, violence, disaster, and sorrow. You've been content with your dog stories for like thirty years now, how about asking for another bone?

How about requesting morality testing for FCC employees? How about checking and balancing media networks again and holding them accountable for their failures toward the public? Why don't people act more like they used to? The "banksters" who leverage the almighty dollar beat down all who stand in the way of profit.

As a whole, society has become non-confrontational—if it don't apply, let it fly. The excuse is that since no one forces us to watch television or listen to the radio, why get upset about it? The shameful thing is that most people are no longer interested in getting involved in anything that might require an investment of time.

In the New Testament, the authorities that captured Jesus were going to kill him at the requests of the people, because the public did not like what he was doing—spreading all his goodness and such. The governor knew Jesus wasn't doing anything wrong and offered the people a choice. He could free Jesus—the good guy—or he could free this other dude who was basically a murderer and all-around bad guy. The people chose the bad guy and the rulers listened. Remember that all trends and changes are started by just a few people. Let's rise to the occasion and start a trend of being righteous. When you see something happening that you know is wrong, take a stand and say something!

CHAPTER 14:

There Is No "I" In Family . . . Oh Wait

I was an only child to my father and I admit that my grandparents slightly spoiled me. Like most children, my thoughts were most always about my own needs. This self-centered attitude is sometimes considered cute, but the child eventually becomes an adult and is no longer cute.

A particularly happy moment from my childhood was driving my baby sister (from my mom's second marriage) home from the hospital. I remember instantly feeling love toward this baby and knew that her needs were now greater than mine. It was also nice in a way to no longer be the center of attention. Although we didn't exactly grow up together, I did enjoy seeing her and tried to bond with her when I could. I can't say that I was always nice to her—and I did tease her on a few occasions—but I was glad to have her in the world.

Sadly, my sister's father apparently had some mental health issues that progressed over the years. In his extreme pursuit of Christianity, he became convinced my sister could talk directly to God. He would sometimes meet with her like some oracle to inquire about the Lord's wishes for his life.

My stepfather believed that God had called him to minister to rural areas of the country—so he quit his job, took flying lessons, and bought a small airplane. While he was doing all this, my mother was paying all the bills on credit cards. After more than a year of this, the family was more than $100,000 in debt. My mom snapped, rightfully so, and left with my sister and younger brother to stay with friends.

As the supposed head of the household, my stepfather neglected to perform his obvious and true mission of providing for his family—all under the pretense of serving God.

In addition, once my mom left, he made no genuine effort to reconcile and never even saw his children again. My mom did the best she could raising her kids. The three of them scraped by through years of poverty.

Mom still prayed and loved God, but admittedly had a sour taste toward extreme Christianity. As a witness, God did provide for their basic needs, but not much else. I sometimes wonder about my sister's mental or emotional status after going from being the mouthpiece of God Himself, to being abandoned by her earthly father. I can tell you that at the age of eighteen, she ran away from home and did not speak to the rest of us for about five years.

She claimed to be upset that my mother was controlling and allotted my sister's paychecks from her first job toward household expenses. Whatever the reason, those were five miserable years for my mother—time that can never be gotten back. I sometimes think about the Prodigal Son who takes his inheritance and leaves the homestead. What if the father had died in the son's absence? A few years after my sister came back, my mom was stricken with breast cancer. Her sickness was left untreated for a couple years due to a lack of health insurance and she had secretly resigned herself to the assumed fate of death. As a pure miracle from God, a treatment option became available and she has now fully recovered from a stage-3 infection. There is no guarantee that any of us will wake up tomorrow, but many people still take time with family for granted—and sometimes even avoid each other for various reasons. Time is really all we have to give of ourselves to show love. I struggle with selfishness in sharing my time with anyone, despite being aware of how short life is. In some ways, as a son, I have failed both my parents by denying them time and communication. Every child has a duty to honor a parent and, eventually, the roles of caregiver will probably be reversed. Be aware when this time comes and do your duty to look after your parents as they first looked after you. Take the time to show your love while you can—otherwise the feelings of guilt will haunt you the rest of your days when a supposed loved one is gone.

CHAPTER 15:

It Takes Money to Lose Money

In the mid 1990s, I realized that the Internet was here to stay and I took the initiative of learning a new skill. I was never much of a technophile, but I taught myself the basics of web page and graphic design in just a few months during my spare time. In the interest of practicing these new skills and making some money on the side, I ran small ads in the local paper. I was basically offering my beginner-level ability at fast-food level pay in exchange for the experience. Although I had no problem selling my service this way, my technical expertise was still limited and my delivered results were sometimes less than satisfactory.

Most people want more than their money rightfully buys and will always complain—even if you give them something for free.

In several instances, I spent a couple weeks doing a project for a hundred bucks or so—only to have my balls busted for not producing results on par with what a Fortune 500 firm might have. I got tired of telling people why they could not have a website just like Amazon.com for five hundred dollars.

After getting a few projects under my belt, I thought about taking the business further. I got together with a coworker from my day job and we started a small company. Our first mistake was that instead of offering a specific quality computer service at a reasonable rate, we attempted to do most anything computer related, offering average quality work and cheap prices to make the sale easy. We had the worst customers you could imagine—the cheapest people, with the least understanding of technology, with the biggest dreams.

Some of these people were so unrealistic that we had to cancel the agreement from our end, and we even gave a few refunds just to get away from further obligation. Some customers felt as if they owned us for a thousand dollars—as if they had bought a tech slave at the market. They would call me sometimes late at night on a weekend, practically demanding a solution or suggestion to their minor concern.

A business-owner's book I once read said to make sure you pay yourself first as you are the most important employee of the company. If only I had kept this wisdom in mind, we would not have taken most of the projects that we did. I gradually improved my business contract writing skills and began to include a "no-satisfaction" clause to protect us from the unrealistic expectations we faced.

During this time, my partner successfully "cut in line" and acquired ourselves a two-letter domain name, which I was able to sell for $100,000. For those unfamiliar with the Internet, a URL is sort of like a phone number in that you only own it while you are paying for it. There used to be a short period of time when a name would be in web-limbo between registration fees and could be snagged by someone paying attention to this. Since then, the Internet gods have gotten smarter and web name properties are not nearly as valuable as they once were.

In any case, we suddenly had an unexpected bit of capital to expand our business. At the time, we were very proud of this white-collar hustle. Even though our maneuver was not exactly criminal or anything, I now realize that ill-gotten profit will be repaid with blackness on your soul. Although the penalty for wrongdoing may not come back to you in this life, the consequences for your spirit should be the real concern.

In the Bible, Judas betrayed his master for money. After the events unfolded and Jesus was killed, seemingly as a result of Judas's actions, Judas wound up hanging himself from a tree out of guilt. Numerous crooked executives have been found dead in their expensive homes or cars at the suicidal work of their own hands. If only they had been able to control their greed, realizing that having wealth only makes you want more. I'm sure someone else said this first, but wealth is only as great as the person who holds it. The Bible tells us that we are all just stewards of the things in this life we hold. We're told that everything is on loan from God and it is our duty to give back to His cause from what we have been so generously given.

CHAPTER 16:

The Oldest Profession Gets Upgraded

I mentioned that I advertised my small business in the local city paper. This publication was very liberal and anyone with anything was welcome to place an ad.

Our listing for "web design" would usually appear at the end of "professional services," which was located just above "adult services." This is relevant because, on a fairly regular basis, we would get calls from working girls and their managers.

Or in other terms, "hos" and "pimps." As it turned out, they would happen to see our ad while checking for their own and figured that being in the same publication, we would not object to servicing their needs to facilitate them serving the needs of others.

The common practice was to show current photos of the "models" that could be hired and one of the main requests we received was the taking of digital photography and getting it on the web. Having a weakness for all things sleazy, I was eager to take on these projects. I quickly bought the best camera money could buy and learned to use it. In business, a dynamic company will often expand its services based on existing client demands.

This allows for a bit of trial and error prior to offering said services to the public with no previous experience. I soon had additional specific services to offer to a community that I would have done well to avoid in the first place.

One of our first clients was a woman from Finland who styled herself as an upscale courtesan and adult entertainer. She had a medium build and was mostly attractive, despite being a bit past her prime. My company was tasked with maintaining her pay-subscription-based website, which featured this woman with any other man, woman, or toy she could get her hands on.

Her site was actually somewhat active due to her local whoring and had revenues of several thousand dollars per month. This gave my partner and me the inspiration to start our own adult pay-site—which is a story for later. In the meantime, let me tell you about the work ethic of this Finnish Femme of DC. Ms. Finland was a good whore. She was obviously bipolar or something as she had frequent mood swings, but she loved her job.

She was usually happy and bubbly when we met in person. She came across as being sophisticated and well-traveled, which was seemingly correct. She thoroughly enjoyed anything of a promiscuous nature and nothing was taboo for her.

She was fairly warm and engaging and her eyes lit up when talking about anything related to sex. All in all, she was quite a character. I was honestly not very attracted to her, but I liked her personality as it matched her decadent lifestyle appropriately. I reluctantly performed with her on one occasion, but I sort of felt dirty and used afterward.

Despite the morality issue, I admired this woman as she took her profession seriously and truly enjoyed her chosen career. She did not complain about her lot in life and seemed to make the most of her situation. I'm fairly certain she did not use drugs; she owned a condo, and even had money saved. She did her job well!

Maybe you're thinking: "I'd enjoy my job and be good at it if all I had to do was have sex for a living!" Well, this may come as a surprise to you, but many women don't like to have sex—especially not with fat, old, hairy, smelly man-pigs. I am slender, young, smooth, and clean, yet I have a hard enough time finding companionship in the form of a long-term relationship, which offers far more than a couple hundred bucks. And if you're a woman thinking this and you're not already doing it, get prepared to lower your standards and throw your soul out the window. The Bible says, "He who meets a prostitute is a fool." A proverb says about an immoral woman, "Her feet go down to death, her steps lay hold in hell."

Since I'm not a theologian, I can't really say how bad that is on a scale of 1–10 or anything. For those that argue that the Bible was written by man instead of being inspired by God, do you mean to tell me that the Bible was written by the only forty men in all of history who didn't like whores?

We know that Jesus was a friend to several prostitutes—all of whom came to change their ways in understanding his teachings. Look, aside from the obvious need to procreate, I can't explain why men have such a strong desire for women. I am guilty of such lust and struggle with it daily—regardless of my understanding of what God wants for my life. I simply urge other men to try to resist these temptations of the flesh. I can tell you that you will eventually regret giving in to them, as I do now.

To continue with the story of my immoral business dealings, another client was one of the aforementioned managers of escorts. We were hired to build and maintain a website to display a constantly changing lineup of available companions. It was understood that, as partial compensation for our time, we could coerce or pay the models for personal services as desired.

I would show up with my fancy camera and some lighting to whatever cheap hotel I was directed to. I was usually able to convince the girls to do full nude sessions and more, saying that it was part of their portfolio for their new job.

In the interest of creating content for my own personal adult website, I became more than a little friendly with numerous women in this arrangement. In maybe two years, I hustled and filmed over a hundred girls from this business relationship. For the most part, you would not want to spend any length of time with—or even know—most of these girls. Although some were levelheaded, most of them were emotional wrecks who abused drugs and alcohol.

Over time, I watched the manager run his escort business. A large part of his job was keeping tabs on the employees. Standard operating procedures would be to plant these destitute girls at a hotel and move them every few days to keep the police from stinging his customers.

His other main task was to answer his three cell phones. Whether it was 3:00 p.m. or 3:00 a.m., he was really pretty good about taking the calls. He was fairly upbeat and professional when speaking to clients. He was also good about putting new girls to work right away and I was often pressed into service on short notice. In fact, I would even show up to meet a new girl and would sometimes have to wait in the car a while as the girl had business of her own to take care of. Since there is little quality control in this industry, he was not above bait and switch. Of course, when the transaction was completed, it didn't really matter what color her hair was.

As a whole, that man understood his business and did his job well. He took the insane drama and bullshit in stride as if it was any other job, like taking orders for pizza.

From a legal perspective, he knew the tricks and stayed under the radar. He never grew the business to anything more than he could personally manage—it would have fallen apart otherwise. I speak of this manager now as I would later meet others of his kind who fell short of his work ethic.

Despite the nature of the business, he took it seriously and prospered. I should mention that his former partner was shot dead over a drug issue with some ho's dealer, so this is certainly not a business a sane person should desire to be a part of. I regret working with people like this. I became a peddler of smut and debauchery. For those of you who think it might have been fun, I can assure you it was usually quite depressing.

I met people in desperate situations—many of whom I took advantage of, making their lives even worse. In conclusion, I went from a legitimate programmer to a pornographer with just a few poor decisions. When people asked me what I did for a living, I had to omit many details, which should have been a sign that what I was doing was wrong. Heed your conscience and listen—and pay even more attention when it says things you don't want to hear. Growing up, I knew that drugs and drinking were bad for me because it was something you heard about. No one ever told me how addictive pornography and sexual promiscuity was, hence I didn't think I was doing anything wrong by engaging in it. If I had only had my nose in the bible instead of a dirty magazine, I would have learned that sex outside of marriage was wrong.

CHAPTER 17:

Try Drilling a Hole in His Head

After my father died, I took the advice my family was giving and went to see a mental health doctor. I did not like the idea that my brain might be broken, but I knew that I probably was a little off center as I generally did see some things differently than perhaps the majority of other people.

I put the consultation off for months because my insurance did not cover mental health. In fact, many insurance companies don't cover MH issues as their underwriters feel that it is too vague an area with few legitimate testing methods and prognosis results.

This may have been true fifty years ago, but for profit's sake, the insurance industries have failed to update its policies. There are now many recognized methods for identifying and treating the brain. A scanner-test called SPECT imaging will clearly show abnormal activity in most cases. In addition, there are many modern tests to detect possible chemical imbalances and such. The reality of the situation is that insurance providers *do* know how real mental health issues are. They also know that some such issues require medication and treatment that become a never-ending process.

Many disturbed individuals go untreated due to this lack of insurability. American jails are overflowing with people who would be just fine with a bit of Prozac. An example of such a case is my neighbor's son. I would almost always see BJ standing in front of their townhome when I was coming or going. He was usually smoking a cig and drinking a beer with a blank look on his face. I would sometimes wave and he would sometimes wave back if he noticed. As a typical suburban American, I never went out of my way to be overly friendly for fear of exactly what happened next. I came home one day and, feeling a bit social, I walked over to BJ to officially introduce myself. He told me his name and we shook hands, but he didn't seem to be much of a conversationalist, so I excused myself after a bit of small talk. Going into my house, I was fairly certain that BJ was a bit lacking in mental agility.

Having a slight aversion to such people, I noted that I would keep my interactions to waves and brief hellos. The next day, within a few minutes of getting home, I heard a knock at the door. I opened it and found six feet and two hundred pounds of a black man staring at me. I will admit to being somewhat intimidated by people of color, but the fact that he was just standing there speechless made it really uncomfortable.

I said, "Hey man, what's up?"

"Nothing," he said. "Just came over to see what you were doing."

After the bit of awkwardness had passed, I remembered my manners and invited him in. He asked where I worked and, after I told him, he asked if I could get him a job anywhere. I asked him what he could do, what types of jobs he had done in the past, and what type of work did he want to do. His response to all three questions was "whatever." At this point, my first impression that he was not running on all eight cylinders became validated. I have a bit of anxiety to blame, but I was really becoming uncomfortable having this man in my home.

I basically told him something along the lines that I would have to think about it and maybe ask around, basically a blow-off had he recognized it as such. He asked if I had anything to eat or any beer. I honestly had neither and opened the refrigerator as proof. I dug out a frozen TV dinner and stated that I had some work to do in an effort to excuse myself. To my relief, he got the message and left after a few final words.

The next day, a few minutes after walking in the door, the knocking came again. BJ wanted to know if I had found him a job yet. I, of course, hadn't even thought about it that day and mentioned that he himself would be best suited to the task of job hunting.

I told him that I would keep my eyes open, but I really didn't know of anything offhand. Two days later, BJ came knocking to check on me again. This time, I held him at the door during our bit of uncomfortable small talk. I got rid of him by explaining that I needed to clean some stuff up before my wife got home. Later, I told Melaney what had been happening with our neighbor. She made light of the situation and said that I was being racist and that I should be kind to BJ as he sounded harmless.

Over the next week or so, he came to the door numerous times, sometimes knocking for a solid ten minutes or more. I did not share my wife's appraisal of the situation and decided that I simply did not want to be friends with BJ. I suppose some of it was that I was white and he was black, but mainly because I was smart—or at least of average intellect—and he was simply not the brightest crayon in the box.

111

As a result of what I now realize was flawed reasoning, I rarely spoke to BJ if I could not avoid it at all. He would sometimes ambush me when I got out of the car, but I used speech and body language to let it be known that I didn't really want to chat. I caught up with his mother one evening and spoke to her about all this. She confided in me that BJ did in fact have some mental issues and was supposed to be taking medication for them. She explained that her insurance did not cover said medications and she could simply not afford them. She worked two jobs and was always gone from like six in the morning until ten o'clock at night. I believed that her financial situation was probably
really tight.

She said she would speak with him about it and apologized for any grief he might have caused me. Things were quiet for a few days—but the following week, the knocking started again. I answered the door and BJ was once again asking about the job that I had supposedly promised him. In an exasperated voice, I told him that I just didn't think I could do anything for him.

Another day, I came home filthy from the shop and jumped in the shower. When I went into the bedroom wearing nothing but boxers, BJ was standing at the foot of the bed, hands in his pockets. Apparently I had neglected to lock the door on my way in. I somehow managed to keep my cool and resisted the urge to shoot him—my .357 was within reach under the bed. As before, I had to speak first.

"What are you doing up here?"

"Jus' checkin' on ya."

"Dude, you really shouldn't just walk into people's houses uninvited."

"Yeah, I thought about that."

"Look dude, you gotta go—you kinda scared me and you could really get into trouble for something like this."

Fortunately for both of us, he quickly left.

When the next knock came a few days later, I finally gave up and called the police. I explained the entire history to the officers. I told them that I mostly worked from home and he was disturbing me. I explained that I simply did not want to be friends with him and didn't know how to handle the situation. I had of course told BJ in a roundabout way that I did not want to be friends, but given his decreased mental capacity, he just didn't get it.

The police spoke with him and I hoped that I had seen the last of him. Being my next-door neighbor, this was just wishful thinking. The next day, the back window of my car was smashed and a side mirror was knocked off. I was angry and a bit frightened, knowing full well who had done it. A few days later, my wife's car was also vandalized. I proceeded to get a restraining order on this fucker, but once again—he lived right next to me. I immediately went out and purchased a video recorder and camera equipment. I stuck a camera above my doorjamb, overlooking the parking lot, and hooked up a motion light to shine right on my car. The very damn day the system was connected, the very hour in fact, we recorded BJ vandalizing our spare third car, which I was driving while the other was in the shop. I called the police and showed them that he was in violation of the newly issued restraining order.

BJ was arrested on the violation with a destruction of property charge. We went to court and were awarded the actual damage costs of $900, which of course, the insurance company had already paid to me. On a related note, the fucking insurance company called me several times a week to turn over this judgment to them in an effort to get their money back from the perpetrator. Since comprehensive claims usually have low deductibles, they'd harass dead deer in the road to pay them back if they could.

A few days after the judgment, my wife came home and found the front door glass smashed with the door open. When she heard a noise in the house, she got back in the car and called me. I told her to call the police. The fuzz showed up in record time—believe it or not—and I got home just a few minutes later. I arrived to the scene of BJ being escorted out of my house in handcuffs. The police showed me the items and money he had in his pockets—mine, of course—and got my background testimony for the reports. Looking around the house, it was obvious that BJ had actually been inside poking around for some time. Drawers were opened or dumped, papers were scattered, and closets were ajar. This was no smash and grab—it was a deliberate and personal violation.

So having caught BJ red-handed, (the only time the police seem to take action), they arrested him.

Over the next few weeks, my wife and I met with the state attorney to push for the maximum sentence. We even appeared in court to testify that this was not a random B&E and not the first problem we'd had with this guy. We also explained to the court that BJ had mental health issues, in the hopes that at least the state would check him out during his incarceration. I don't know how much help he wound up getting on the inside, but he did serve about four of the five years given to him. The time went by quickly and he currently is sitting on his front stoop, smoking his cig, and drinking his beer. Thus far, I have not had any problems with him, but of course we are now both on probation after my own stupidness, so maybe that makes us more alike than different. From a Christian perspective, I think back on the whole encounter. Had I loved my neighbor, maybe none of this would have happened. I failed at my neighborly duties when I placed judgment on this human for both his skin color and his learning disabilities. How hard would it have been for me to be kind? Perhaps I really could have made some small effort to find him a job.

I could have even gotten to know him better before writing him off from being a potential friend. Even after the situation had climaxed, I still could have shown forgiveness and not have gone to court against him out of anger. In summary, because this man could not get his "happy pill" for lack of insurance coverage and finances, the taxpayers had to incarcerate him for four years at a total cost of like $120,000.

I also see how his own mother failed him by not making his medication a priority—regardless of the cost. Sometimes I think about how far humanity has come and then I realize that we are only a few steps ahead of drilling a hole in someone's skull in order to let the demons out.

Insurance in any form is just plain ugly.

We are bullied into having it out of fear or—in some cases—by law. We are reminded that if we died, our families would starve—unless you killed yourself, in which case they would get nothing. We are required to have insurance for business liability and even to register a car. Yet make one or two driving blunders and your policy will be canceled for sure.

Automotive insurance and medical insurance are tracked more vigorously than the FBI's most wanted list. Your driving record and your ailments are constantly updated in secret database files that the insurance companies trade like baseball cards, but even with safe driving and loyalty discounts, your premiums continue to rise each year.

Years ago, I had a cracked water pipe behind my wall that slowly leaked for a few days before I noticed it. There was drywall damage and mold had even started to grow on my carpet. I attempted to make a claim to my homeowner's policy. They first rejected the claim, stating that my home was technically a condo and was covered by a master policy through the HOA. After reviewing the bylaws of the HOA, such damage was not covered and was to be directed to my homeowner's tab. They reluctantly accepted the claim, but rejected it within a week. Not only did they reject my claim, but I got a letter the following week stating that my policy was being canceled. The letter said, "We regret that we can no longer insure you due to the fact that you recently made a claim. Our research shows that people who have made one claim are likely to make future claims as well. Based on these statistics, you are too high risk for us to insure. Thank you for your business."

WTF, I thought I was supposed to be in "good hands." Instead I was surrounded by grabbing hands that wanted my annual something for nothing. My fear of loss motivated me to pay ten dollars per month, which was only good for theft (a fire claim would have fallen under the master HOA policy). Even then, I learned that I would have had to have kept receipts for any stolen items to be claimed as lost.

Of course, the one B&E I have experienced in my whole life happened after this policy was canceled. I learned that water damage requires a whole other type of insurance policy that you have to ask for. Maybe most people know these things and I'm just ignorant. Or maybe the insurance companies rely on our ignorance and our aversion to reading dozens of pages of microscopic print!

In this instance, I failed as a consumer to properly educate myself. Many people buy insurance, (among other things), simply because they are required to.

Did you know that auto insurance companies will "suggest" the amount of coverage you need when you request a quote ? These amounts are usually more than the state minimum, which you have to specifically ask for in order to get the lowest price. But the grabbing hands of these devils usually open in mock honesty as they remind you that if you total someone's new luxury car, you could be liable for more than your house is worth. Scare tactics are a proven way to market a service.

Insurance companies are not totally wrong for having their fine print contracts. When I took my vandalized car to the repair shop, here's what happened. Both side mirrors had been knocked off and I had bought junkyard replacements. I could have done it myself, but I needed something else done to the car and took it to the shop. Upon learning that I was using insurance for the work, the guy sends the car off to another shop to have the doors painted—without even telling me. There was barely a fucking scratch on the paint, but these assholes decided that if insurance was paying, it was reason to totally repaint the doors on a fifteen-year-old car. The doors were painted a damn half-shade whiter than the rest of the car—had I not been so stressed about other issues, I would have gone back and made them paint the whole damn car. In any case, the total cost to screw on two fucking mirrors and paint two doors was close to $1,000. The whole damn car wasn't worth much more than $1,000! I should have just requested an estimate and pocketed the money, but I just told my shop to take care of it. The shop got almost a grand, and the insurance people got a $200 deductible as well as a year's worth of no prior claims. As a consumer, I totally failed to demand satisfaction here.

After 9/11, insurance companies quickly devised "terrorism coverage" as another way to soak the policyholders through fear. So now, for an extra 10 percent, we no longer have to fear terrorists or an act of God!

CHAPTER 18:

Pay or Just Go Away and Die

Knowing that my insurance did not cover mental health, I walked into the psychiatrist's office like a man preparing to cross a desert with only a half-empty cup of water. The "gatekeeper" informed me that the hourly rate was $200 and asked me how I planned to pay. As we all know, "medical receptionist" is just a fancy title for cashier.

So I laid two C-notes on the desk and sat down to wait. A few moments later, I was sitting in front of someone who looked as if he could have been Sigmund Freud himself. He was about a hundred years old and of some ethnicity I could not identify. He asked me how I felt. I assumed he wanted me to answer with more than a token "just fine" response, so I gave the question some thought. I told him that I was sad that my father had died, my marriage was a farce, and I felt a total lack of purpose in life. Something changed in his eyes and, for a moment, I thought I saw either dollar signs or perhaps concern. He asked me to tell him about myself. Not knowing where to begin, I gave him a *Reader's Digest* story of my life. There really wasn't much to tell; my life has never held much in the way of extreme tragedy or elation.

When our hour was up, I felt I had given the doctor a good insight into my background and problems. He folded his hands and informed me that I probably had a mild bipolar disorder and would benefit from drug treatment. I knew about the term bipolar because my wife had the condition, but my thought patterns were nothing like hers!

I could only assume that—with a half-dozen degrees and certificates hanging on the wall—this man knew what he was talking about and wasn't making a random diagnosis.

I was sort of under the impression that determining someone's mental condition would usually require some kind of testing. But the doctor opened a large metal cabinet with an entire pharmacy's worth of psychotropic medications. There was enough Prozac in there for an entire high school cheerleading squad!

How did this guy come to acquire such a large supply of serious drugs? I'd think that recognized pharmaceutical companies would not have to keep giving out free samples of drugs that have been on the market for twenty years.

In any case, he loaded me up with a month's supply of Depakote and Cymbalta and sent me on my merry way with a second appointment in three weeks. I took the pills he gave me, but they seemed to make me more edgy than anything else.

I wasn't really pleased with his prognosis and, after maybe four visits, I stopped seeing the doctor and taking the medications. A year later, a more formal diagnosis of my mental faculties (in jail) determined that I had mild to severe generalized anxiety issues. The new doctor did not think I was bipolar and I was prescribed Celexa (like Prozac) for my treatment. Although my circumstances at the time were very stressful, the pills actually did make me feel better in just a few weeks.

The message in this story is to find a doctor (regarding any illness) who is willing to spend time with you prior to entering a treatment course. Even elite private doctors are overbooked and pressured to make judgment calls based on time restrictions and insurance limitations.

In addition, today's lawsuit-happy patients hinder doctors from using many modern treatment options. Instead, they resort to thirty-year-old drugs that may have unknown side effects.

Even as patients, we are still customers, and must make ourselves aware of available treatment options. I saw a commercial where someone was buying a cell phone and asks a million questions about it. Then that person goes to the doctor and, when asked if there are any questions, the person had not a one. One time, my dad and I went to his general practitioner whom he had selected from a book years earlier and had seen maybe twice previously. The doctor actually took over the home office of another doctor that had retired. The office looked like a third-world clinic. The walls were discolored in places where papers or posters had obviously been hanging for many years, but had been recently removed. The laminated medical diagram charts had dates on them from the 1970s. The furniture would have been rejected and thrown away by the Salvation Army. This so-called doctor failed to diagnose my father's bone cancer and blamed his aches and pains on a previous fall and told him to take aspirin.

Many people, my dad included, will only go to a doctor if they think something is seriously wrong. I think we need more doctors who are actually interested in seriously examining people as opposed to just doing the minimum to earn a paycheck. Instead of citing a Bible story that talks about health care and insurance, let me suggest the following. In the Old Testament, people used to live for close to one thousand years and now we get sick and die in less than a hundred. I have heard that this is a sign of the spiritual distance we have travelled away from our Creator. Seeing sickness and death should be a reminder to us all how short life is and help us to focus more on spending our precious little time in God's will.

CHAPTER 19:

One in a Million

In my business dealings, I have had the pleasure of working with one of the most decent and honorable men—next to my own father. For close to five years, I worked at a specialty auto garage and my job was selling car parts on the Internet. Tony, the owner, was my boss. Although I wasn't actually a documented employee and he did not issue me weekly paychecks, I treated him with respect just the same.

Not even counting his dealings with me, I have heard and seen the equitable treatment Tony gave to customers large and small. In fact, prior to working at his shop, I was a customer as well.

When I first met Tony, I was the new owner of a fairly old car. I had just brought the car over from another shop where a friend of mine worked and I had already spent several thousand dollars in repairs. Another friend who owned a similar car had previously recommended Tony's shop, but had told me that Tony was expensive and you usually had to make an appointment several weeks in advance. In the hopes of saving money and getting quick service, I went to the place where my other friend worked first. Let me tell you—not only did my friend's shop keep the car for over a month, but I still spent a shitload of money and half of the work they did wasn't done correctly. In addition, they neglected to do a bunch of the things I had requested.

Needless to say, Tony's shop was very understanding of my plight and took me in right away. I saw that this specialty shop rate was actually less than the discounted rate my friend had given me. In addition, seeing a whole row of cars the same as mine in the parking lot, it dawned on me that working on essentially the same type of car all the time would take the specialty shop less time to diagnose and fix a given problem.

I'm sure we can all remember times when we've taken our cars to mechanics and described the funny noise, smell, or vibration to give them a clue as what to fix.

The usual response is that they'll need to look it over because the problem could be one of several different things. At Tony's shop, 90 percent of the time, they knew exactly what the problem was before the car even went on the lift. Based on all this, I quickly began to appreciate the value of going to a specialist.

In an industrial complex full of automotive shops, Tony's is the only one that's busy nonstop and books appointments a month in advance. The idea of a garage that works on only one type of car is both insane and brilliant at the same time. Tony had realized that man's first sin of pride would drive the better customers through the door. He and his staff had a true passion for the cars being serviced—and a desire to do things the right way. Aside from wanting customers to be happy, the guys at the shop complete even little jobs to the best of their abilities.

Even when nobody else would notice that a corner had been cut, the guys made sure every screw was properly threaded. Lastly, Tony treated other people better than he knew he would ultimately be treated in return. His estimates and timeframes are accurate, and he always delivers as promised or better. Although Tony is not openly religious, he is a good example of someone who lives and works as the Bible defines the way a Christian should. Knowing that he is a Christian, I see the correlation—his business has been blessed beyond what just his own efforts might have otherwise brought.

Even as a pessimist and a former non-believer, the workings of God made an impression on me through how this man ran his business. You see, most people just don't give a shit and draw a line as to how much they are willing to give for a fee. Tony was always concerned about his reputation first and—even in instances when he would have been in the right to have blown off a customer—he went the extra mile. I hope that other supposedly Christian business owners will read this testimony and remember to trust their success to the Lord.

CHAPTER 20:

Someone for Everyone

When I was fresh out of high school, my dating prospects were either dismal or nonexistent.

In those days the Internet was still in its infantile stages, and being under twenty-one prevented me from doing the bar scene. Of course, meeting people at a bar never seemed that appealing since the only girls not with someone else were either neighborhood sluts or lesbians (which is what men call women when they reject us).

My options for meeting dates were limited to work, the mall, or through friends. Considering some of my friends were gay, and the rest were as dorky as I was, that just left work or the mall. In hindsight, if I had to do things over, I would have gone to church to find my dates. As it was, I worked at McDonalds, and even the lady with a visible mustache had a boyfriend.

So I was pretty much reduced to meeting girls at the mall. I did spend a good bit of time at the mall, between the video arcade and the dungeons and dorks game store. The real game was trying to talk to girls from the high school just up the street. The nice thing about being a young guy is that you at least don't creep out the young girls.

One thing I will say about meeting girls back then—even having no money, no car, and no class—it was still easier to talk to the opposite sex than it seems now.

My first girlfriend was a well-developed fourteen-year-old of Italian descent. After hanging out with her a couple times, I finally managed to get her over to my house one day. What's a little messed up is that I actually ditched the other friends I was also hanging out with across the street to get this girl alone. I quickly figured out how everything worked and finally lost my virginity to this girl whom I had known for like four days. The sucky part is that time flies by when you're screwing and, as I was going for round three, my dad came home.

My dad probably wouldn't have been so pissed about the girl in my bed, but my friends had made their way back to my house and were busy drinking his beer in the basement. Needless to say, he was super-pissed, but I think he at least understood.

A few days later, I took my sweetheart to a friend's house with plans to stay there with her that night. I don't think her trailer-trash parents gave a damn about her whereabouts because her dad or uncle or whatever had seen me making out with her in the car a few days prior and didn't even stop walking to the front door.

Jen and I (I think that was her name) proceeded to get busy in my friend's bed in the basement while my two buddies were upstairs watching MTV.

My great night of debauchery ended when my friend's mom came downstairs early the next morning to do laundry. You'd think she had never seen two naked teenagers before and started screaming like she had seen a mouse or something.

We basically had to leave and wound up hanging out at my other friend's house for a while and then I took her home—not because I wanted to, but I was actually a bit worried about what her parents were thinking.

The relationship lasted another week or two until Jen introduced me to one of her slightly hotter and older girlfriends, Erica.

The day I met Erica, I bought her a smoothie at the mall and then took her out to my friend's car in the parking lot and screwed her right in the back seat. I basically had to break up with Jen—pretty unceremoniously, I will add—and proceeded to date Erica. We went out for a whopping three months before she dumped me for some reason—maybe for not having a car of my own.

She wound up dating my best friend—who had his own car—for like three years or so. It was a bit awkward when the three of us would hang out, but I tried to remember the rule of bros before hos and just dealt with it. When you're young, awkward situations just aren't such a big deal.

For reasons I don't really know or understand, my friend hasn't had a date since then—much less another girlfriend—and this happened over fifteen years ago.

For the next five years, I was busy trying to keep a roof over my head and getting a girlfriend seemed like less of a priority. Again, had I continuously been attending a church, I know things would have been better during those years.

AFTER YEARS OF SIN... THE WORD OF GOD FINALLY REACHED THE BUNNY RANCH

One biblical concept I learned is that Christians are supposed to love everyone, but give preferential treatment toward others of the same faith. This makes me think that others would have reached out to me during these years—which certainly were a struggle. Simply for showing up to a building for an hour on Sundays, I know that I would have been led to a good job, a decent place to live, and a worthwhile companion. As it was, I stood on my own two legs, which I now know are very weak.

In the big picture, I cheated myself out of a meaningful relationship by being in such a hurry to have sex with the first girl I could get.

There was no love in any of my past relationships. I think many people—let alone young people—are just not capable of understanding real love. The Bible says, "God is love." If this is true, one would have to first understand a bit about God in order to understand love. Yet so many people seek love as if it were its own entity. People love other people, money, sex, drugs, power, or simpler things like music or a sunny day. Yet most of these people are only made happy by these things for a short time and then they want more. So how do you get to know God? He's not just going to walk up and say, "Hey, I'm God—nice to meet you."

The answer to that question is simple and complicated at the same time. Since I might not do such a great job of explaining my thoughts, let me just say that the Bible also says, "If you draw near to Him, He will draw near to you." This means that if you show an interest, He will find a way to communicate with you. I can testify that if you start thinking about what God might want instead of what you want, He will take control of your life and good things will happen. For starters, try attending your local church on Sunday or read a few pages from the Bible each day for a week and watch stuff happen for you.

Another mistake I made was dumping my first girlfriend for the second for no good reason at all. It was the beginning of a clear defect in my character that has continued to grow over the years. For that matter, how worthwhile was the new girl who would allow me to leave the old in her favor? Maybe teenage reasoning is flawed, but character has to start and stop somewhere. Even as young as she was, Jen had some good qualities and probably would have stuck around despite the fact that I had little to offer other than the chance of an unexpected pregnancy.

Fifteen or twenty years later, I am still making the same mistakes. Without a Higher Power to hold them together, it's no wonder most relationships fall apart. Is this not more obvious as we see religion pushed out of daily life and divorce rates climb? Many couples never even get married—and some aren't even totally monogamous.

In a few instances, I've approached a woman to talk and learned that she was "living with someone." What the fuck does that mean? Why not just say "I'm involved" or something. "I'm living with someone" means that a girl pays half the bills and is having sex with some guy without all the hassle of being married. It means she's basically a live-in whore and she knows it—otherwise she would have said something else.

I've heard of girls who live with someone for two or four or six or eight or more years but still have no ring. If a girl had a damn rock on her finger, I wouldn't have approached her in the first place. Wise up, women! You wonder why you're objectified and don't get proper treatment. It's because you have allowed it to become not only acceptable, but normal.

Around that time, I got the idea stuck in my head that, in order to get a woman interested and keep her, I had to have something to offer.

Being a worldly thinker at the time, my ideas of what I could offer revolved around money and security as opposed to something as seemingly trivial as my personal character. This viewpoint was probably further developed by my occasional visits to the nudie clubs. In order to get the stripper to pinch your face with her titties, you first had to have a dollar in your mouth. For the next few years, I really focused on making a bit of money and getting established. As I have already admitted, my thinking was flawed and, if you recognize the same pattern, here is your chance to stop. Having a big house, a fancy car, and nice clothes are not "good qualities."

In addition, dating a woman for her large breasts is a double-edged sword due to all the attention she will certainly get from other men for the same reason. In general, dating someone with the secret hopes that someone "better" will come along isn't really fair to either party. This is one thing that most people are guilty of—myself included.

If you think someone is a couple inches too short to date, maybe you might be a few inches too shallow. Perhaps looking for someone who is just like your last partner is a bad idea as it probably won't work this time either. In summary, if you date or marry someone for superficial reasons, it should come as no surprise when that person leaves you over something equally trivial.

Ignoring the Oedipal reference, young men should look at the good qualities of their mothers and seek out women with the same. Girls should look to their fathers, but refrain from dating men twice their age.

If you live in a shitty neighborhood and all the potential role-models you know are human trash, it's time to meet some new people—and even bad neighborhoods have churches. Before I started on my journey of understanding God, I thought I could do anything immoral and the consequences wouldn't matter. I now realize that even the seemingly unimportant decisions I made in the past have closed many doors.

My current relationship situation is fairly dismal. I have the baggage from all my past poor decisions to lug around like Jacob Marley's chain. The "good" girls don't want me because I'm too jaded, and the "bad" girls don't want me because—despite my baggage—I'm still just "too nice."

Out of loneliness, I wind up talking to women that are either too old for me or so fat that they'd accidentally crush me to death in their sleep. I appreciate larger women more than most, but if I can't carry my girl out of a burning building, it's not going to work.

I still pray every night for God to fix my fuck-ups and I keep searching. I suppose I could do nothing and wait, but I've heard that doing nothing about a situation is a decision in itself. To close, if you're struggling with any issues—in a relationship or otherwise—try praying about it and you might get an answer.

CHAPTER 21:

On the Po-Po

I took a test in college to see what my career interests might be. The results showed that I should pursue a position as an air traffic controller, a bus driver, or a police officer. At one point, I thought it would be interesting to be a cop. As I grew older, I realized that the police were forced to deal with the worst people society has to offer. In addition, it seemed as if it was part of the patrol officer's job to harass people and that the police made most people feel uncomfortable.

The few times I've personally dealt with the police or seen them deal with other people, I got the distinct impression that the cop was assuming the worst. Regardless of who the police officer might be talking to, you just know they're expecting trouble.

I can certainly appreciate that the average police person is subjected to morons on a daily basis, but do they really need to treat everyone like morons? It's been proven that most police will overreact to any given crime—but whether from caution or boredom I can't say.

The few law enforcement people I've known have displayed an "above the law" mentality in words and actions. A police officer that lived next to my friend pulled up in his cruiser one day and proceeded to unload his trunk full of illegal explosive fireworks and light them off in his front yard with his family. Another police officer that lived at the townhouse on the end of my row was caught red-handed falsifying work documents for illegal aliens. A deputy I knew personally told me of his sexual conquests of high school girls. When I worked at McDonald's years ago, the weekend night cop told me how he was getting thirty dollars an hour from the restaurant as well as his regular pay since he was also on duty. I knew a kid whose dad was a cop and the kid sold weed that his dad had confiscated from small-time dealers.

We've all seen the police speeding and turning on their cruiser lights just to run a red light. I mean, I get it—they protect and serve and therefore deserve some special considerations. I really don't care if an officer makes a few extra dollars babysitting some convenience store or runs the occasional red light, but should this behavior really be the norm?

Romans 13 talks about how we must respect and subject ourselves to the authorities in place here on earth. It also points out that these authorities should subject themselves to God's will. The motto of America used to be "In God We Trust." Now it seems that the American government isn't even allowed to acknowledge God—let alone trust in Him. I told you earlier that I had been in jail once. While I admit that my intentions were wrong, the police solicited me and created a scenario that would not have otherwise existed. I would have never done what I was charged with on my own. I certainly did have some problems to work out, but more than a year in jail seems a hard way to learn a lesson. In hindsight, I am glad to have had the time to find God and reflect on all the things that had led me to that point. If at least one person who doesn't know me reads this book and finds God, then it was all worth it.

CHAPTER 22:

A King Needs a Castle

At an early age, I grasped the concept of owning something as opposed to renting—namely one's place of dwelling. A tuxedo is one thing, but renting a room in a house with people I didn't really know just plain sucked.

I can't think of many good reasons that excuse the loss of equity and security that buying a home offers. I've heard a few people say they don't want to be "rooted down," but that just sounds like an excuse for not having their shit together.

At the age of twenty-five, I worked at a mortgage company and learned how easy it was to buy a home. I learned that our government wants Americans to own homes and created the Federal Housing Authority. This agency makes it possible for almost anyone to qualify for a home loan and achieve the American Dream.

When I applied in 1998, I had a 587 credit score (not good) and I had earned less than $40,000 the year prior. Despite these less-than-stellar qualifications, I was able to buy a home valued at $90,000 without putting a single penny down. In fact, when I went to closing, the seller wrote me a check for $300 to cover some water stains on the drywall from a small leak that had been fixed.

Ten years later, I have replaced almost everything at a cost of another $60,000 and it's very nice. For a total of about $150,000, I now own a great place that has appreciated to a value of nearly $300,000 (and depreciated back to 150 thanks to the housing market crash). Had I been renting the past ten years for $500 a month, I would have pissed away $60,000 with nothing to show for it. As it stands, I basically lived the past ten years rent-free due to the appreciation of my house.

I didn't really know much about money or real estate, but I knew that buying a place of my own was a good thing to work toward. If you work at McDonald's and can't qualify for a home, you should make an effort to improve your employment situation.

Thinking about how crazy the economy has been, it would also be wise to make sure the timing is right and you're in a position to get what you want for a reasonable deal. It's funny to think about all the "smart" people who bough shoebox houses in expensive neighborhoods for a million dollars via interest-only loans. Sometimes you need to look at the big picture and realize that something is just too expensive. If enough people had refused to pay such high prices for homes that were clearly not worth it, the housing market might not have collapsed the way it did, dragging the rest of the economy with it.

Another Bible story that comes to mind is the one about Moses leading the chosen people to the Promised Land in Exodus. The Jewish people had a poor quality of life and were basically slaves in Egypt because they were not living according to God's will. But God still loved them and wanted to give them a better life. The Lord made a path for them to start over, but the Israelites kept screwing it up along the way, despite the effort that was being made on their behalf. In the end, it took them forty years to travel a distance that could have been crossed in a few months—all because they wanted to do things their way and not God's. One of the lessons I learned from this story is that God will provide for your needs when you do things His way. Although I managed to buy a home via mundane channels, the whole process could have been better if the Lord had been prominent in my life at the time. Within months of moving into my house, just about every appliance broke and I had a number of plumbing problems. Most people would write this off to coincidence or the facts of life, but I can't help thinking that if I had let God pick my house, I wouldn't have had so many problems right away.

If you think about it, just being able to work a job is a gift from God that facilitates buying a house in the first place. I could give you some examples of how I currently see God looking after me, but you might miss the point and think that it's all about what God can do for you. I'm certainly no theologian or holy person so all I can say is that seeing is believing. My hope is that I've at least piqued your interest into how you can have a better life through a relationship with God and I encourage you to check out your local church and pick up the Bible sometime. Obviously, many of the concepts in this book do *not* represent Christian values. If you think about it, most of the humor here is funny because it is plain sad to know how some people—like myself—have lived their lives. In the end, writing this book is by far the greatest thing I've done with my life. If just one life is changed and just one soul saved, my life will have had meaning. If you want to talk, send me an email: mikeisverycool@ yahoo.com. I don't deal well with endings; with that said, see you later.